Hello!
I am a fox.

I0108773

Foxes are mammals and belong to the dog family.

Foxes are about 2 to 3 feet (less than 1m) long.

A group of foxes is called a "skulk," "leash," or "troop."

I love my "skulk."

There are about 37 different species of foxes around the world.
The most common type of fox is the red fox.

We rely on our parents to care for us when we are young.

Baby foxes are called "kits".
They born blind and deaf.

Foxes are very social animals.

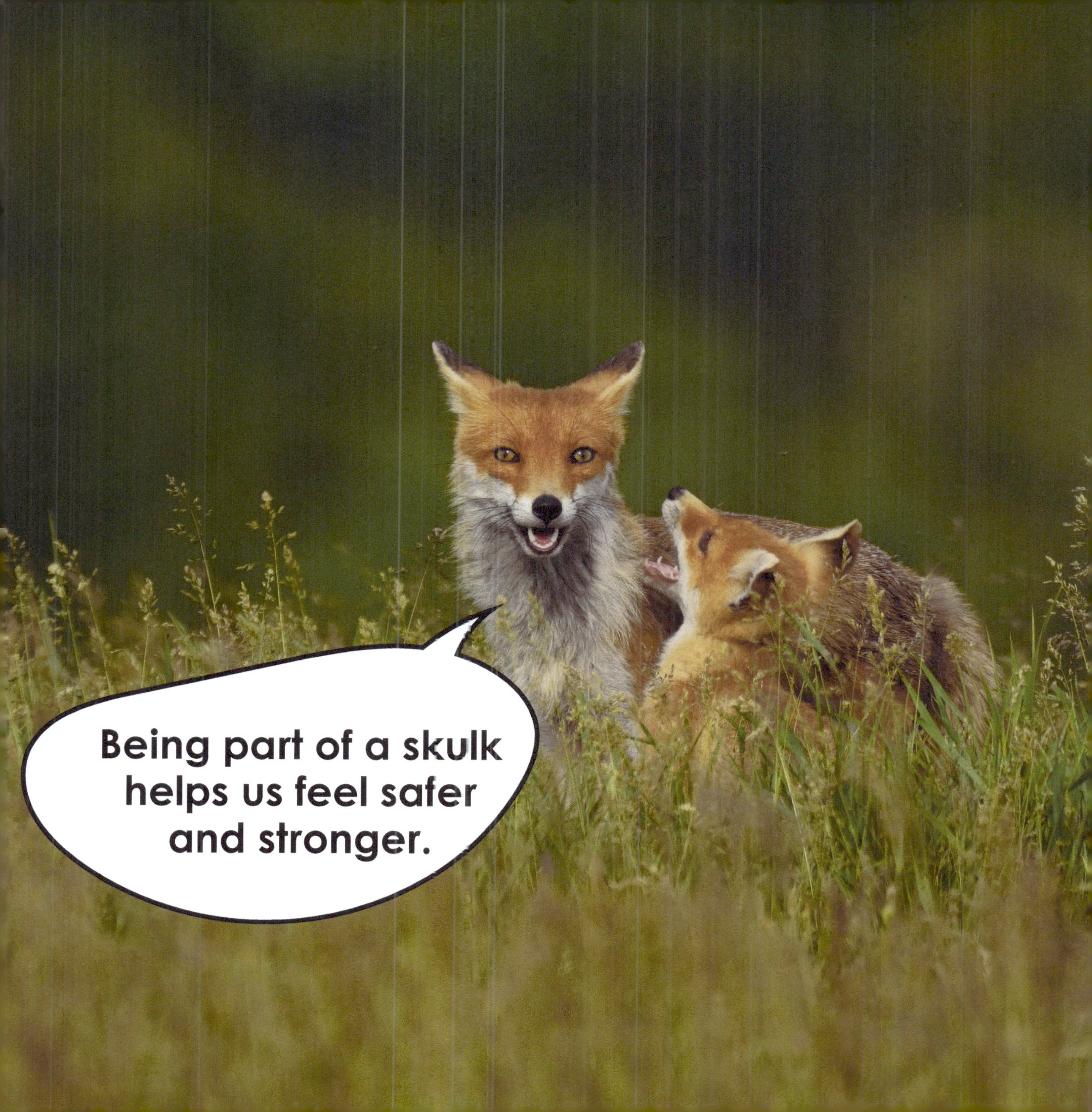
Being part of a skulk helps us feel safer and stronger.

Foxes are nocturnal animals.

How a fox looks helps it survive and thrive in different habitats around the world.

A fox can jump up to 4 feet
(about 1m) high.

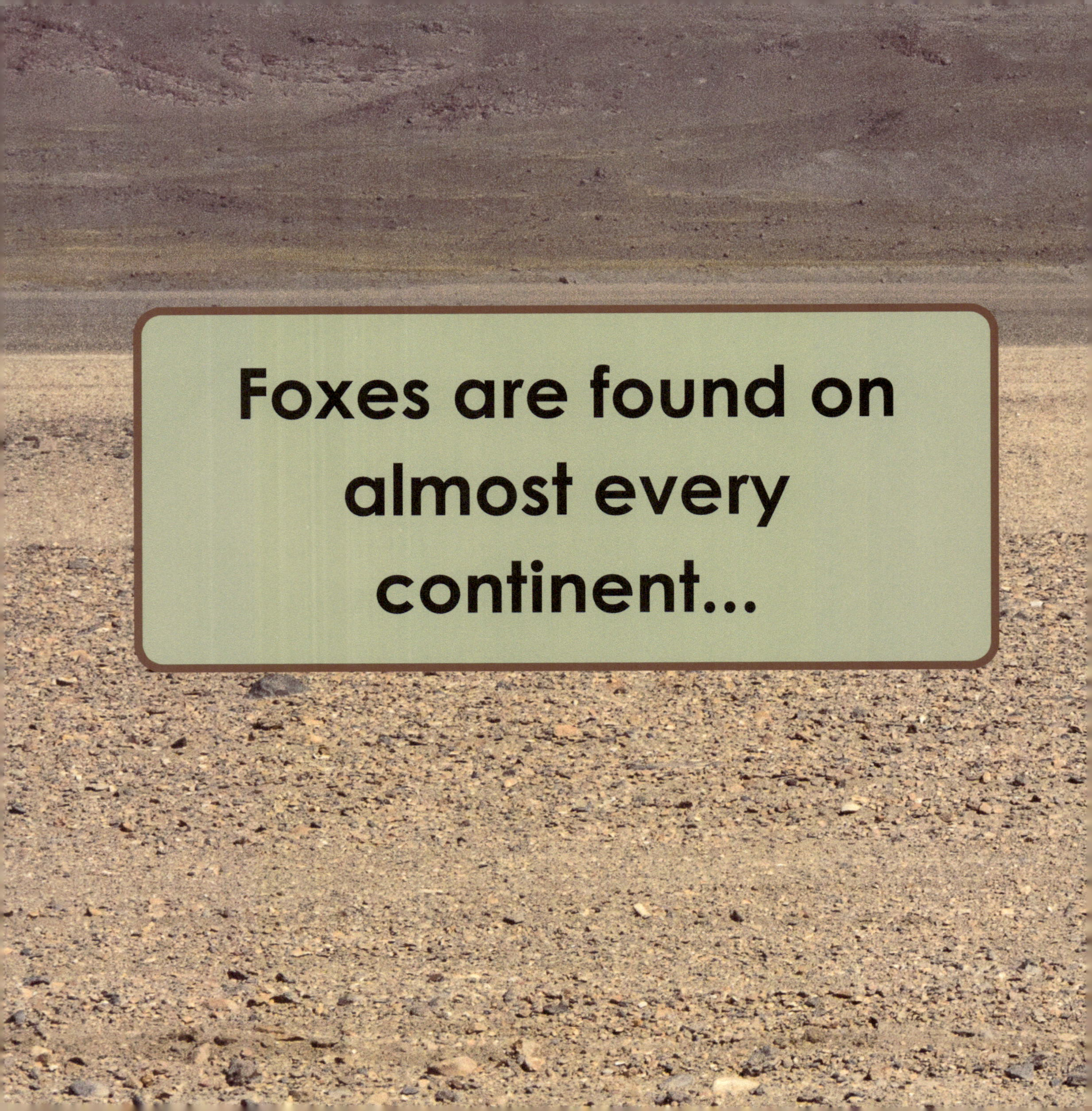

Foxes are found on almost every continent...

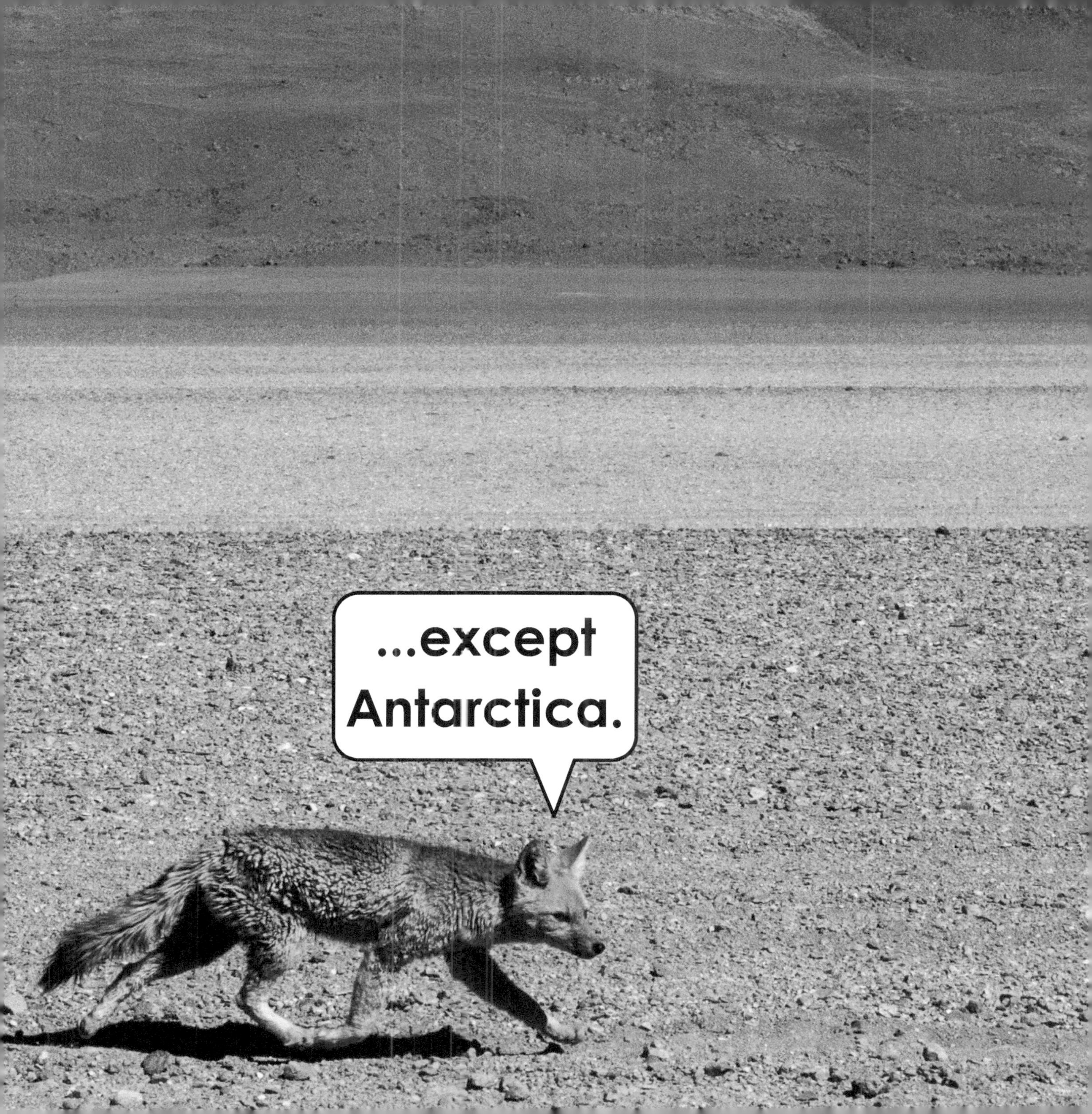
...except Antarctica.

Foxes are excellent swimmers and can paddle through water.

Some foxes, like the gray fox, can climb trees to escape predators or find food.

Foxes can run up to 30 miles (48 km) per hour.

Foxes are known for their curious and playful behavior.

They often engage in games with each other.

What's up?

Foxes have a wide range of sounds, including barks, howls, and screams.

Foxes communicate by using scent marking and body language.

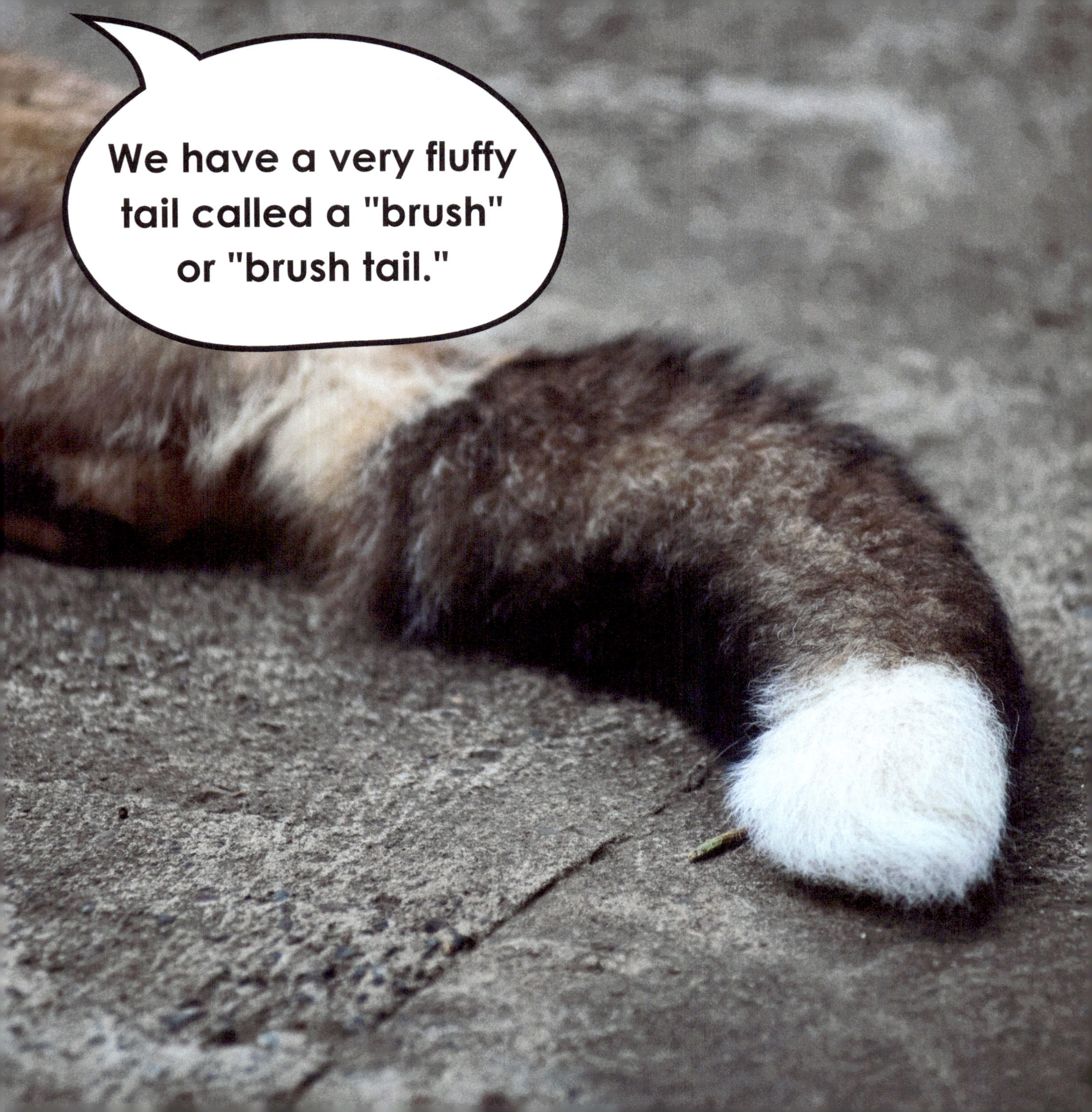
We have a very fluffy tail called a "brush" or "brush tail."

I use my whiskers to explore.

Fox whiskers help them feel and sense things in the dark.

Foxes eat a variety of foods, such as rodents, birds, fruits, and insects.

Foxes have dens, which are like their homes, where they rest, and sleep.

We raise our kits in the den too.

Fennec foxes have large ears that help them stay cool in the hot desert.

You cool?

Yeah, I'm cool.

Arctic foxes have thick fur and a bushy tail they use as a blanket.

I can survive in very cold weather.

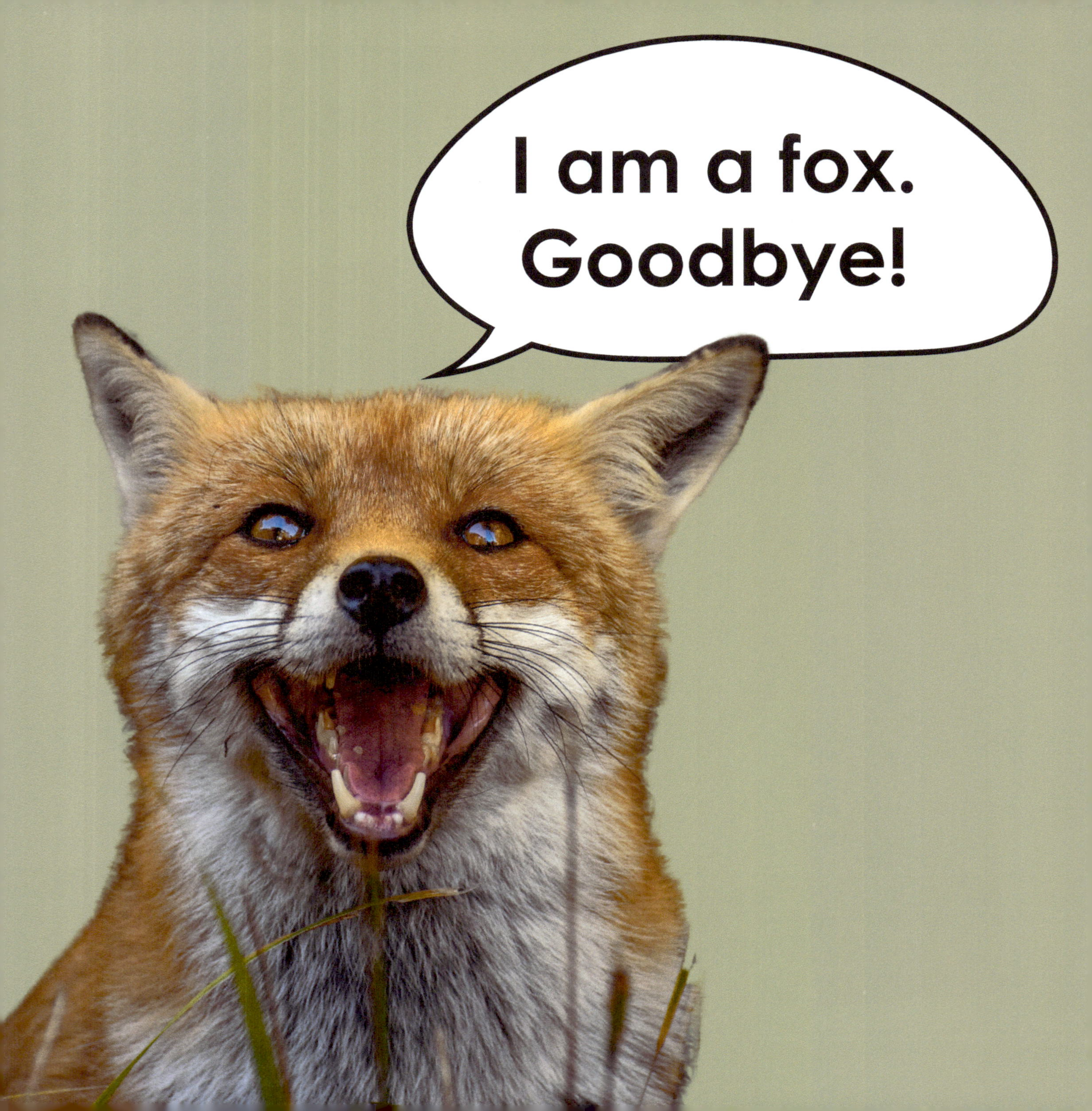
I am a fox.
Goodbye!

Want more?

| I am a Giraffe | I am a Lion | I am a Polar Bear | I am a Turkey | I am an Octopus | I am a Spider | I am a Border Collie |
| FUN GIRAFFE FACTS & PHOTOS | FUN LION FACTS & PHOTOS | FUN POLAR BEAR FACTS & PHOTOS | FUN TURKEY FACTS & PHOTOS | FUN OCTOPUS FACTS & PHOTOS | FUN SPIDER FACTS & PHOTOS | FUN BORDER COLLIE FACTS & PHOTOS |

| I am a Tiger | I am a Goldfish | I am a Snake | I am a Shark | I am a Fox | I am a Chicken | I am a Wolf |
| FUN TIGER FACTS & PHOTOS | FUN GOLDFISH FACTS & PHOTOS | FUN SNAKE FACTS & PHOTOS | FUN SHARK FACTS & PHOTOS | FUN FOX FACTS & PHOTOS | FUN CHICKEN FACTS & PHOTOS | FUN WOLF FACTS & PHOTOS |

| I am a Deer | I am a Bear | I am a Horse | I am a Bee | I am a Beaver | I am a Penguin | I am an Ant |
| FUN DEER FACTS & PHOTOS | FUN BEAR FACTS & PHOTOS | FUN HORSE FACTS & PHOTOS | FUN BEE FACTS & PHOTOS | FUN BEAVER FACTS & PHOTOS | FUN PENGUIN FACTS & PHOTOS | FUN ANT FACTS & PHOTOS |

| I am an Elephant | I am a Rabbit | I am a Turtle | I am a Tortoise | I am a Reindeer | I am a Llama | am an Owl |
| FUN ELEPHANT FACTS & PHOTOS | FUN RABBIT FACTS & PHOTOS | FUN TURTLE FACTS & PHOTOS | FUN TORTOISE FACTS & PHOTOS | FUN REINDEER FACTS & PHOTOS | FUN LLAMA FACTS & PHOTOS | FUN OWL FACTS & PHOTOS |

| I am a Panda | I am an Ape | I am Dangerous | I am Polite | I am LOVING |
| FUN PANDA FACTS & PHOTOS | FUN APE FACTS & PHOTOS | FUN FACTS & PHOTOS OF THE WORLD'S MOST FIERCE ANIMALS | FUN FACTS & PHOTOS OF THE WORLD'S MOST COURTEOUS ANIMALS | FUN FACTS & PHOTOS OF THE WORLD'S MOST WARM-HEARTED ANIMALS |

... and more

COLLECT THEM ALL!

ActiveBrainsBooks.com

Hello parents!

Visit us to find out about new releases and *FREE* offers. We'll let you know when we have a new release coming out and how you can get it for FREE.
And you can cast your vote for what book we make next!

scan here

or visit here

ActiveBrainsBooks.com

---

scan here

Let us know what you think. As an independent publisher, your honest reviews mean a lot to us and our business. We'd love to hear from you!

amazon.com/review/create-review/

or visit here

FOLLOW US on Amazon.

amazon.com/author/activebrainsbooks

ACTIVE BRAINS

ActiveBrainsBooks.com

www.ingramcontent.com/pod-product-compliance
Lightning Source LLC
Chambersburg PA
CBHW042056040426
42447CB00003B/251